TS 2

READING SKILLS FOR LEARNING

Dorothy Brogden

Thomas Nelson and Sons Ltd
Nelson House Mayfield Road
Walton-on-Thames Surrey KT12 5PL UK

51 York Place
Edinburgh EH1 3JD UK

Thomas Nelson (Hong Kong) Ltd
Toppan Building 10/F
22A Westlands Road
Quarry Bay Hong Kong

Distributed in Australia by

Thomas Nelson Australia
480 La Trobe Street
Melbourne Victoria 3000
and in Sydney, Brisbane, Adelaide and Perth

First published by Thomas Nelson and Sons Ltd 1983
Reprinted 1984 (twice), 1985, 1986, 1987

ISBN 0-17-412367-1

NCN 12-JEN-0733-06

Set in Linotron Meridien and Univers by Western Printing Services Ltd, Bristol
Printed in Hong Kong

To the teacher

This series of five books has been designed to help children develop the skills which are essential if project or topic assignments are to be worthwhile activities.

When a child embarks upon topic work we are asking him to carry out three main activities:

1. to extract information from a variety of sources.
2. to interpret, adapt and reorganise the information in order to meet the needs of a particular purpose.
3. to present the information as a summary.

The summary should be the pupil's own work and to some degree, framed in his own words. To attain this end the pupil must analyse and reorganise the material he has collected and present it as a coherent and cohesive whole. The final result should be an original piece of work, drawn *from* various sources but *in* none of them. This is a difficult task for the majority of children but it can be made easier by systematic practice of the specific skills involved.

To give practice in the skills is the particular aim of this series of books. In each book there is a skills analysis chart which indicates the progression of skills from classification to extraction and reorganisation of relevant facts. More detailed information about the specific skills and their progression can be found in the introduction to the Answer Book which accompanies the series.

	SKILLS	OBJECTIVES
INFORMATION SEARCH	Enquiry. An ability to define goals and initiate search. Classification. Alphabetical order. Use of dictionary, directory, atlas, timetables, reference books. Reading strategy.	Extraction
CONCEPTUAL UNDERSTANDING	Use of models – diagrams, plans, tables, maps, flow charts – as an aid to comprehension. Progression in use of models: 1. interpretation 2. completion 3. construction	Reorganisation
SUMMARY	The collocation of the reorganised material.	Presentation

Acknowledgements

The author and publishers are grateful to the following for permission to reproduce the material included in this book: William Collins Sons & Co Ltd for the extracts from **The Return of the Witch** by Margaret Stuart Barry; Macdonald & Co (Publishers) Ltd for the extract from **Cowboys** © Macdonald & Co (Publishers) Ltd 1971, and the extract from **Whizz Kids, Birdwatching** © Macdonald Educational Ltd 1979; Basil Blackwell Publisher Ltd for the extract from **Cowboys** by T. A. Thompson.

The Publishers have made every effort to trace copyright holders of reprinted material. Any errors or omissions will be corrected in future impressions.

Illustrations

Illustrations appearing in this book have been prepared by: KAG: pages 4, 5, 6, 7 left, 17, 18, 19, 27, 31, 34, 44 left, 45; Pauline King: pages 7 right, 21; Sara Silcock: pages 9, 10; Tony Morris: pages 14, 15, 33; Toni Goffe: pages 43, 44 right; Maggie Ling: pages 36, 37.

Series design by Richard Crawford. Cover by Richard Wheatley.

Photographs

Barnaby's picture library (pages 4, 30); Peter Newark's Western Americana (pages 12, 13); Chris Perrett (pages 22, 35, 41); Sporting pictures (UK) Ltd (page 26); Keystone Press Agency (page 46).

Contents

UNIT 1

Sailing

A

1. Look up the definitions of the words below and write them in your book.
The first one has been done for you.

port The left hand side of a ship or boat or aircraft, looking forward.
starboard
bow (of a boat or ship)
stern (of a boat or a ship)

2. Below is a drawing of the hull of a boat.
Copy it into your book.
On your drawing mark:
the bow, the stern, port, starboard.

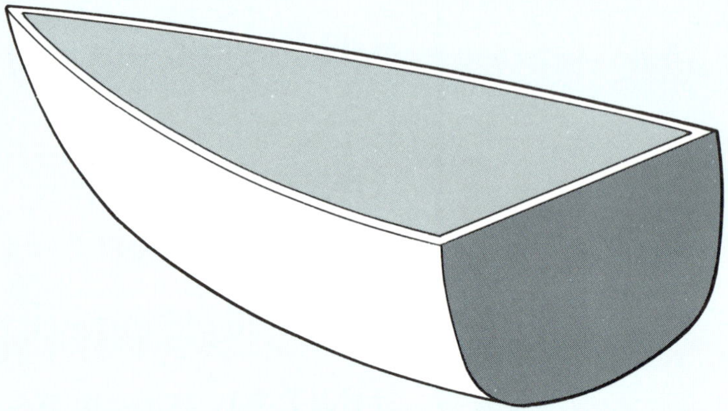

Using a dictionary.

B Look at the six parts of a sailing boat listed below. Four of them have definitions taken from a dictionary.

hull The body or frame of a ship or boat. Masts, sails and rigging are not part of the hull.

mast

sail

rudder A moveable flat piece at the rear end of a boat or ship by which it is steered.

tiller A bar or handle used to turn the rudder in steering a boat.

burgee A special flag which is used to show the direction the wind is blowing. It is attached to the top of the mast.

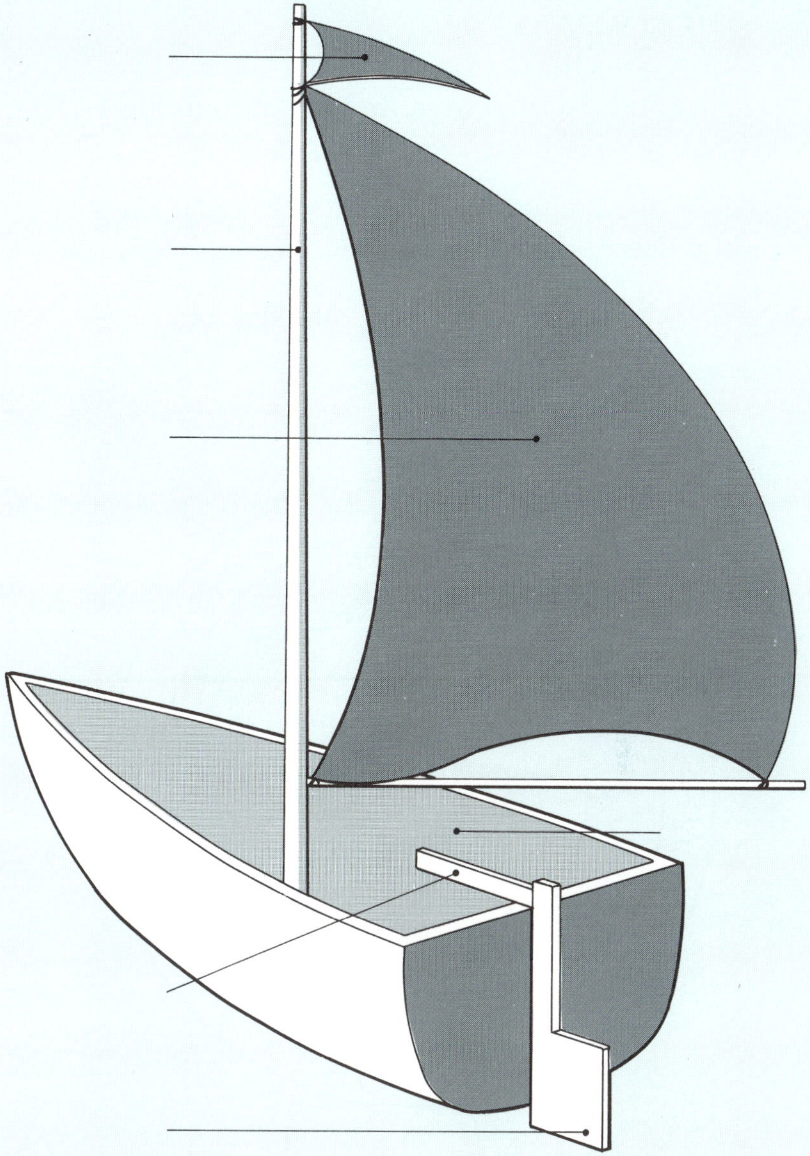

1. Look up the definitions of a mast and a sail. Write them in your book.
2. Copy the drawing of a sailing boat into your book. Use the definitions above and the definitions that you have found to help you name the parts.
3. Name two things which move a sailing boat through the water.

C THE COMPASS

Far out to sea, out of sight of land, sailors use a compass to help them steer in the direction they wish to go.

Look at the diagram of a compass below. It shows eight different directions in which a boat might sail. Use the compass to work out in which direction the boats in the diagrams on the right are sailing. Question **1.a.** has been done for you.

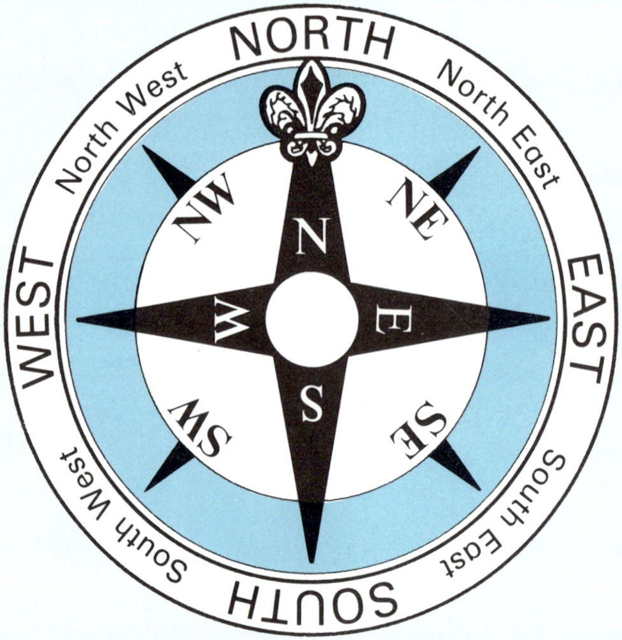

1. **a.** This diagram shows a boat sailing north.
b. This diagram shows a boat sailing □.
c. This diagram shows a boat sailing □.
d. This diagram shows a boat sailing □.

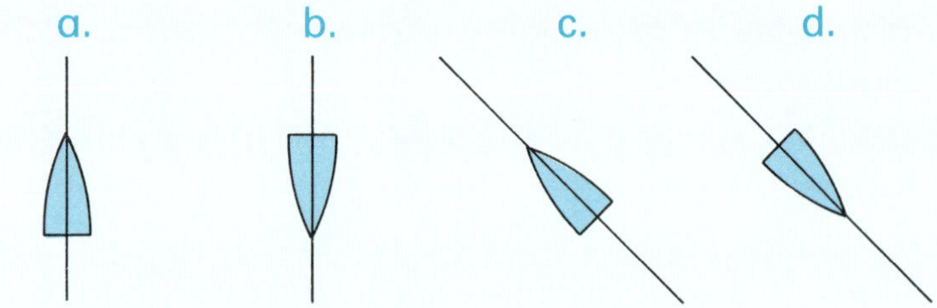

2. Draw these diagrams:

a. A boat sailing west
b. A boat sailing north east
c. A boat sailing east
d. A boat sailing south west

3. In which direction are the boats below travelling? The first one has been done for you.

a. The boat is travelling north and then north east.
b. The boat is travelling □ and then □.
c. The boat is travelling □ and then □.
d. The boat is travelling □ and then □.

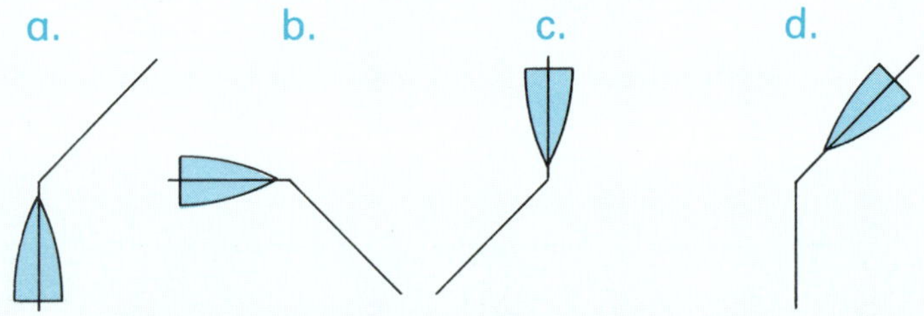

Interpreting diagrams.

D BURIED TREASURE

A compass can help you to find the way on land as well as at sea.

If you follow the directions below you will be able to draw Devil's Island and find the treasure that is hidden there.

First take a piece of squared paper. Copy the grid below on to your piece of paper. Make sure that each side has 12 squares. Mark in the compass directions and the start.

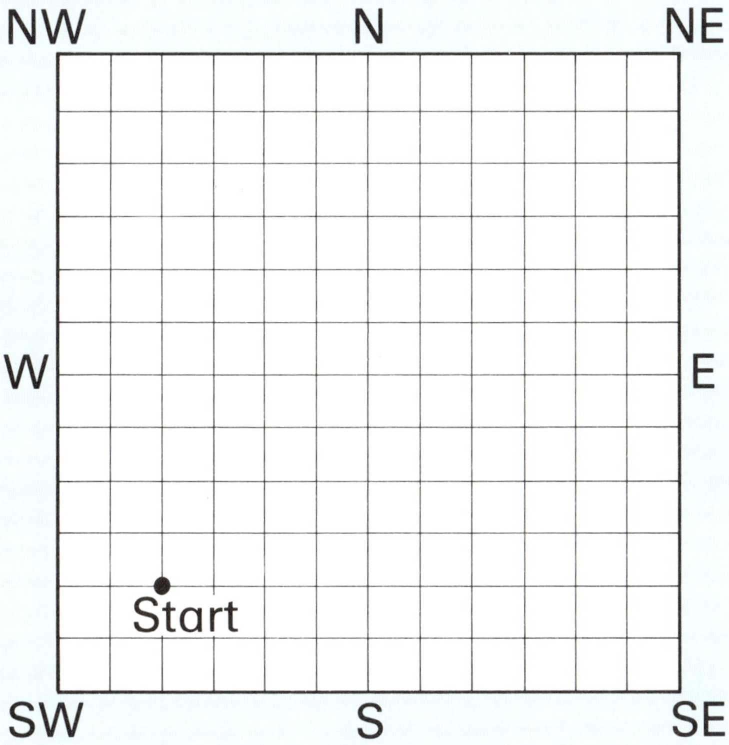

Now draw Devil's Island by following the directions below. Begin on **start**.

1. Move 2 squares NE
2. Move 1 square N
3. Move 3 squares NW
4. Move 2 squares N
5. Move 2 squares E
6. Move 1 square NE
7. Move 3 squares E
8. Move 1 square SE
9. Move 1 square E
10. Move 1 square S
11. Move 2 squares NE
12. Move 1 square S
13. Move 1 square SW
14. Move 1 square SE
15. Move 2 squares S
16. Move 1 square SW
17. Move 1 square S
18. Move 2 squares SW
19. Move 1 square W
20. Move 1 square SW
21. Move 1 square NW
22. Move 3 squares W

Now that you have drawn Devil's Island you can find where the treasure is hidden. From the most southern point of the island go 4 squares North and then 2 squares North West. Mark the treasure point on your map.

UNIT 2

Which Child?

This is a quiz game. You have to find out which child the quiz master is thinking about by looking at the children on the opposite page and asking questions.

In the first round the answer was found by asking three questions only:

Questions	Answers
boy or girl?	boy
dark or fair?	dark
long or short trousers?	short

Answer: Child number [8]

You will find the other rounds on the page after next. They all have parts missing. Copy each round into your book and complete it. Try to ask no more than three questions.

Enquiry. Asking appropriate questions. Redundancy in questions. Scanning.

1.

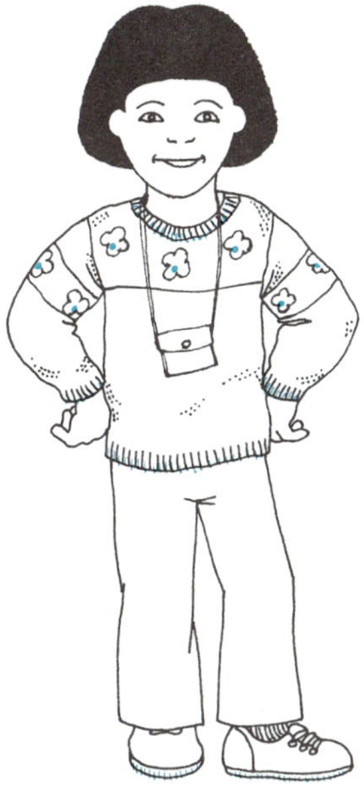

2.

3.

4.

5.

6.

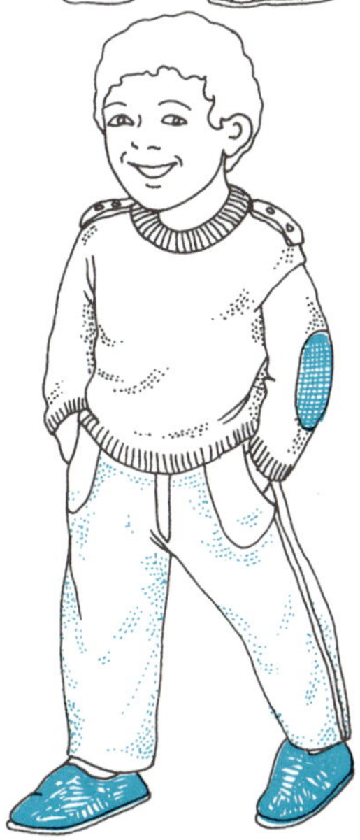

7.

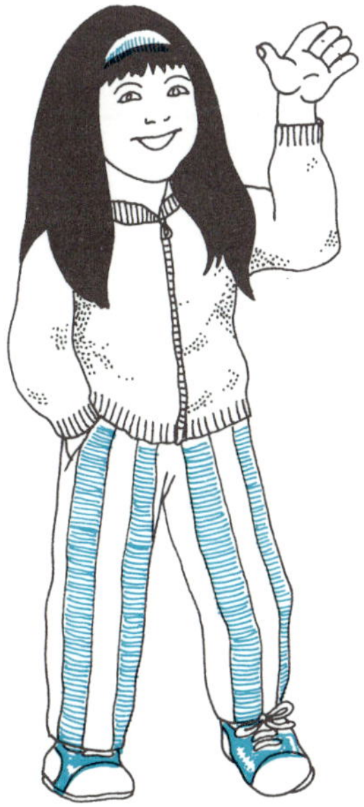

8.

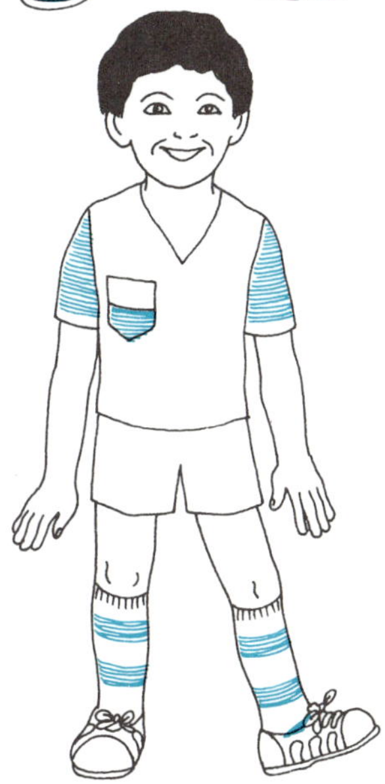

	Question	Answer
1.	dark or fair?	dark
	boy or girl?	boy
	long or short trousers?	long

Answer: number ☐

	Question	Answer
2.	boy or girl?	girl
	short or long hair?	short
	______________?	______

Answer: number 1

	Question	Answer
3.	fair or dark?	fair
	______________?	______
	______________?	______

Answer: number 6

	Question	Answer
4.	short or long hair?	long
	______________?	______

Answer: number 4

	Question	Answer
5.	trousers or skirt?	trousers
	______________?	______
	______________?	______

Answer: number 2

	Question	Answer
6.	______________?	______
	______________?	______
	______________?	______

Answer: number 3

7. Has this child been described already? No

Answer: number ☐

8. Now copy the table on the opposite page into your book and use the information you have collected to complete it. Each line should have four ticks in it and the child's number.

Enquiry. Asking appropriate questions. Redundancy in questions. Scanning.

Which child?

Number of child	Sex		Hair				Clothes		
	boy	girl	fair	dark	long	short	long trousers	short trousers	skirt
7		✓		✓	✓				
2	✓		✓			✓		✓	
		✓	✓		✓				✓
8	✓								
5				✓					
		✓		✓			✓		
				✓					✓
6									

Classifying. Analysing information and presenting in an alternative form.

UNIT 3

Cowboys

In this unit you will read three passages from books about cowboys. Read each passage carefully and then answer the questions underneath.

A In the early days it was a hard job getting the cows to the markets where they were killed. It was no good killing them on the ranges because there were no lorries or railways to carry the meat. The cattle had to be driven in a large herd a long way to the towns where they were needed. The cattle were rounded up and those to be sent away were kept on the trail. The herd was not made to move too quickly. If the animals rushed along they would get thin and not be worth much at market.

From *Cowboys* by T. A. Thompson

1. If you read the text carefully, you can find two reasons why cattle and cowboys spent a long time on the trail. What were the reasons?
2. If animals are to be killed a long way from the market where the meat is to be sold, there is something else that is needed besides lorries or trains. What is it?
3. What is the *main idea* of this passage? If you were to give the passage a title, what would it be?

Inferential comprehension. Main idea.

B Horses were trained in different ways. One man would "bust" them, another would "gentle" them.

"Busting" was making a horse behave as its rider wanted by busting or breaking its spirit. This was done by forcing it to do whatever was wanted.

"Gentling" a horse was training it by being kind and gentle to it. The cowboy would speak quietly to the frightened animal to make it calm, and he would stroke its body softly. In this way the horse would become used to men. Gentling took longer than busting, but it was kinder.

From *Cowboys* by T. A. Thompson

1. Which was the cruel way of training a horse? Why was it cruel?
2. What was the main reason for *not* training a horse by gentling?
3. Write down the *main idea* in this text. What is the text about?
4. Write down the important details in this text. There are two.

C The big holiday for the cowboy was when the rodeo was held. All Americans have a holiday on the 4th July, and many rodeos are held on that day.

The rodeo gave the cowboy a chance to have a good time and see who was best at doing things such as riding a wild, untrained pony, or bucking bronco as it called.

Other prizes were given for lassoing, for doing tricks on horseback, for branding, for riding on the back of a cow, and for many other things. Many of these were dangerous. Men were often hurt at rodeos, but they thought this was all part of the excitement.

From *Cowboys* by Stephanie Connell and Vivienne Driscoll

1. What is a rodeo?
2. Why do you think many rodeos are held on the 4th July?
3. What was one of the dangerous things a cowboy would do at a rodeo?
4. What is this text about? Write down the main idea.
5. What are the important details in the text? The details tell you what the cowboys do at the rodeo. Can you find five things?

UNIT 4

Fables

Here are the beginnings of four stories. The order of the sentences in each story has been muddled up.

Sort out the five sentences in each story into the right order. Do not copy the sentences into your book. Just rearrange the letters by each sentence to show the correct order. Then write the letters down in your book.

Sequencing. Recognising syntactic and semantic cues between sentences.

1. **a.** They kept together for company.
b. Soon there was the sound of heavy footsteps in the undergrowth.
c. Two men were travelling through a wood to reach town before nightfall.
d. Suddenly a great brown bear stood in the pathway in front of them.
e. It was getting dark.

2. **a.** But at last it was near the time when he would die, and he wanted to teach his sons how to be good farmers.
b. So he called them to him one evening and said, "My boys, it may be that I haven't much longer to live. But before I die, I want you to know that there is great treasure in my vineyard. Promise me you will remember that when I am gone."
c. He had done very well for his wife and their three sons.
d. He wasn't at all sure that they really knew how important it is to work hard.
e. There was once an old farmer who had worked all his life growing grapes in his vineyard.

3. **a.** One goat strayed away from his companions to get at some fine long grass that grew a little distance from the path.
b. A boy was following them, trying to get them to move faster, as he wanted his supper.
c. "Get back!" shouted the boy. "Get back, there, I say!"
d. A herd of goats was being driven slowly home to be milked.
e. But the goat took no notice.

4. **a.** Cat was always on the prowl.
b. They had been having a dreadful time lately. They never had a moment's peace.
c. So one day the mice met together in a safe dry cellar to talk about him.
d. It seemed that his owner did not give him enough food. He was always hungry and hunted for mice day and night.
e. You can understand that the meeting of the mice was a very angry one.

UNIT 5

Making Plans

In this unit you will be asked to read some passages and then to draw plans from what you read.

A Read the passage below, then look at the plan on the opposite page. It shows the table where Mrs. Hall and the children were sitting. Can you work out where Wayne was sitting?

Mrs. Hall left the blackboard and went to sit at the table where five children were working.

"How far have you got?" she asked Jon.

"I have just started my drawing," he replied, but I am waiting to borrow Susan's red felt-tip." (Susan was sitting next to him on his right.)

Rachel and Carl were working together and sharing the same book.

"Rachel, move your chair a little closer to me and let me hear you read," said Mrs. Hall. "You take the book you were sharing with Carl. He can share with Jon for a few minutes. Wayne, that looks a good piece of work. I'll see it when I've heard Rachel read."

1. Copy the plan into your book and complete it to show where the other children were sitting.
2. At the bottom of your plan copy this sentence and complete it:

Wayne was sitting between □ and □.

Inferential comprehension. Completion of a plan to help understand a text.

B Four children in Mrs. Hall's class lived in the same block of flats. The block was four floors high.

Alan lived on the top floor and Elena lived on the floor between Pam and Nick. Nick lived in the flat below Elena.

1. Draw a diagram of the block of flats in which the children lived.
2. Show on which floor each child lived.

C Peter always looked forward to staying with his grandparents. They lived in a bungalow and Peter liked the idea of going to bed downstairs instead of upstairs as he did at home.

The bungalow was small – just right for two old people to look after. As you went in through the front door and into the hall, the sitting room was on the right and the grandparents' bedroom was opposite. Down the hall and next to the sitting room was a lovely big kitchen, the biggest room in the bungalow, where Peter's grandparents ate all their meals. The bathroom was on the other side of the hall from the kitchen. It was between the grandparents' bedroom and the small room Peter slept in when he visited his grandparents.

1. Draw a plan of the grandparents' bungalow. As you make your plan, refer to the text to check that you have got the details right.
2. Give your plan a title and, if necessary, a key.

D Peter's Grandparents lived in a bungalow, but there are many other sorts of house. Look at the picture of different types of house. Then answer these questions:

1. Which house in the picture is a bungalow?

2. How is a double fronted house different from a single fronted house?

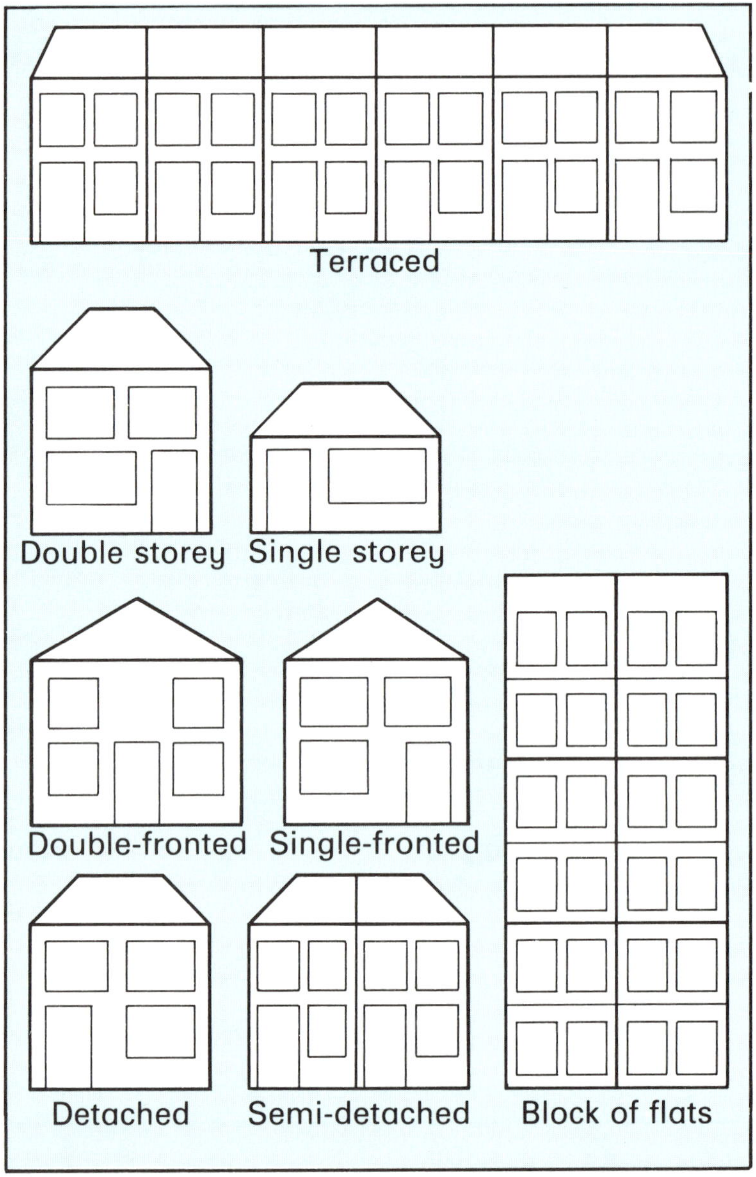

Creating a plan to help understand a text.

3. Look at the drawings of a detached and a semi-detached house.

   a. Write down what you think the word **semi** means.
   b. Draw a semi-circle.

4. Copy the table below into your book. Choose 10 children in your class and find out what kind of house they live in. Record the information on your table.

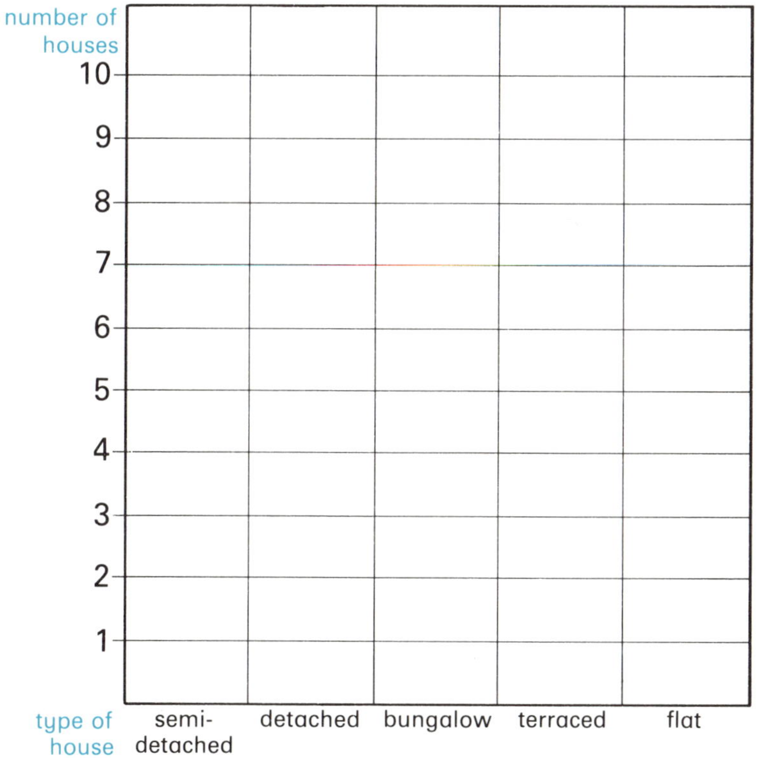

5. Why do most flat dwellers live in towns?

6. **a.** What are the advantages of living in a bungalow?
   b. What sort of people do you think would prefer to live in a bungalow?

7. Which kind of house would you prefer to live in? Give your reasons.

8. Who or what are you most likely to find living in the following places? You may need to use a dictionary.

   a. nest
   b. keep
   c. aviary
   d. kennel
   e. coop
   f. convent
   g. igloo
   h. burrow
   i. hutch
   j. earth
   k. apiary
   l. tepee

UNIT 6

Which Order?

A Here are seven questions asked by a detective, and Bill's seven answers to the questions.

The detective's questions are numbered and Bill's answers are shown by letters.

Find Bill's answers to each of the detective's questions and match the letter to the number. The first one has been done for you. Set out your work like this:

1 [b] 2 ☐ 3 ☐ 4 ☐ 5 ☐ 6 ☐ 7 ☐

Detective

1. Did you go past the Big House on Tuesday night?
2. How are you so certain that it was Tuesday night and not another night?
3. What did you notice when you came past?
4. Do you know that the house has been shut up all winter?
5. Then why did you not report that you had seen a light?
6. Did you see anything else besides the light?
7. Didn't that arouse your suspicions?

Bill

a. There was a van in the drive. The light from the window was shining down on it.

b. Yes, I did.

c. That's the night I go to the swimming club and I always come home past the Big House.

d. Yes, I did.

e. It didn't at the time, but I can see now that it should have done.

f. There was a light in an upstairs window.

g. I thought perhaps the owners had returned.

Sequencing. Recognising syntactic and semantic cues between sentences.

B **1.** Now look at these five sentences. They are in a mixed-up order. Write them in your book in the correct order.

a. If they haven't one, bring a white one instead.
b. Will you go to the shop, please?
c. Julie, we have no bread left.
d. Take my purse.
e. I would like a brown loaf.

2. Do the same with these four sentences. Then draw a map to show the way to the circus.

a. The circus is in the field behind the football ground.
b. Turn left by the post office.
c. Go about 400 metres along the road until you reach the football ground which will be on your left.
d. Follow this road until you come to the post office on your left.

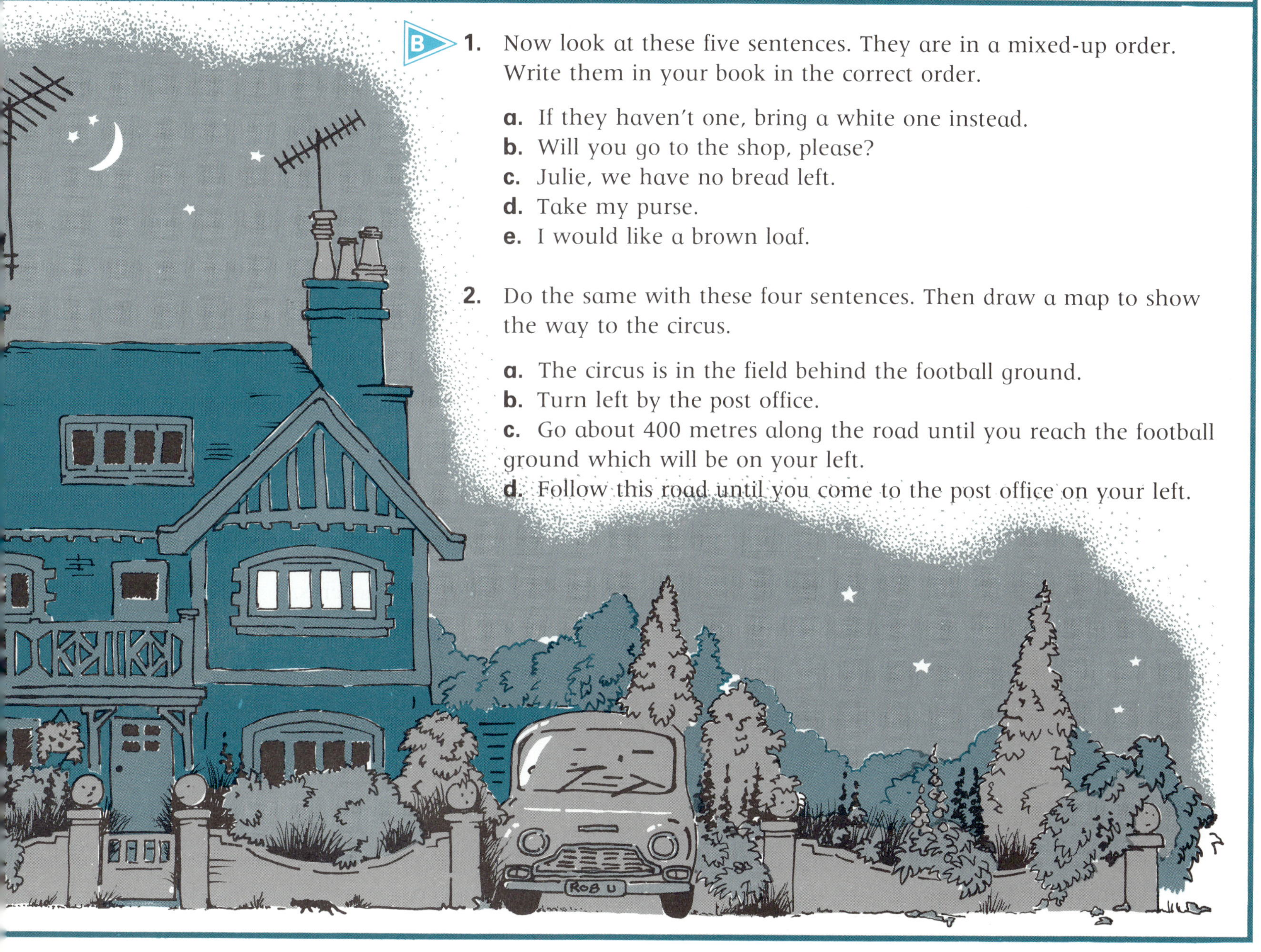

UNIT 7

Connections

A Look at this list:

water, towels, seat, bath, shower.

The things in this list can be found:

a. in a bathroom
b. at the swimming baths

Now read the lists below. Then write the two places where you think the things in each list are most likely to be found. Look back at the example if you need help.

1. shorts, tee shirts, tennis rackets, duffle bags, training shoes.
2. butter, cheese, eggs, milk, cream.
3. oil, wheels, petrol, mechanics, cars.
4. gates, litter bins, seats, climbing frame, children.
5. seats, doors, driver, tickets, passenger.
6. elephant, lion, buffalo, tiger, rhinoceros.

B **WHERE?**

Look at this list:

shorts, tee shirts, tennis rackets, duffle bags, training shoes.

Where might you find these things?
They could be in a sports shop or a changing room.
If you add another word to the list you can make it right for a sports shop but not for a changing room.

For example: cash register or shop assistant

1. Look at the group of words below:

chairs, tables, books, shelves

could be found in either

a classroom **or** a library.

Add a word to the group of words so that the list is right for the library but not for the classroom.

Now do the same with the following groups of words, making the list apply to the word underlined.

2. driver, passengers, engine, doors, windows

could be found in either

a bus **or** a car.

3. field, tents, caravans, cars

could be found in either

a caravan site **or** a fair.

4. cars, lorries, road signs, speed limits

could be found in either

a road **or** a motorway.

C Arrange each list below into two sets of words which are connected in some way.

Then choose one word in the list which you do not know, and look up its meaning in a dictionary. Write the meaning in your book.

The first one has been done for you.

1. look, grin, frown, stare, smile, peep, glance, look.

look	grin
stare	frown
peep	smile
glance	pout

pout: to push one's lips out in a sulky way

2. pal, walk, gallop, friend, canter, partner, mate, trot.

3. leap, float, hop, bound, swim, paddle, jump, wade.

4. afraid, scared, merry, glad, frightened, jolly, cheerful, terrified.

5. titter, blubber, chuckle, sob, weep, laugh, cry, giggle.

6. fling, heave, pull, throw, hurl, drag, bowl, tug.

7. clutch, drop, hold, tumble, seize, fall, grasp, plunge.

UNIT 8

Team Games

Look at the table opposite which gives you some information about team games. There is some more information written next to the table.

Pretend you are taking part in a quiz game and you are given this table to help you find the answers.

1. If the game on the quiz master's card was rugby union, you could get the answer by asking one question only – if you were very lucky and chose the right one to start with. What is that question?
2. If you were told that the game on the quiz master's card was either basketball or netball, what is the only question you need to ask?
3. Suppose the game on the card was hockey and the panel started by asking how many players there are in a team. What would the next question be?
4. If the game was either rounders or baseball, which question must you ask?
5. If the game was football, which is the only question you would need to ask?
6. Use a reference book to find out what a plan of either a football pitch or a netball court looks like.
   Draw the plan in your book.
   Under your plan write the following information:

   Game . . . .
   length of pitch/court:
   width of pitch/court:
   number of players in a team:
   length of each half of the game:

Redundancy in questioning. Inferential comprehension. Interpreting a table. Scanning. Study skills.

Game	Where played		Number of players in a team	Length of each half of game
Football	outside	pitch	11	45 mins
Hockey	outside	pitch	11	35 mins
Shinty	outside	pitch	12	35 mins
Rugby union	outside	pitch	15	40 mins
Rugby league	outside	pitch	13	40 mins
Basketball	in/out	court	5	20 mins
Netball	in/out	court	7	20 mins
Rounders	outside	pitch	9	–
Baseball	outside	pitch	9	–

Other information:
Baseball is played mostly in America and probably came from the English game of rounders. Shinty is one of the oldest British games and it is played like hockey.

UNIT 9

Which Sport?

"Which sport?" is a quiz game. In it a team try to find out the name of a sport written on the quiz master's card by asking him questions.

The flow chart on the opposite page shows the questions and answers in the first round. The questions asked by the team are shown in the rectangles. The quiz master's answers are shown in the circles. The team started the quiz well but in the end they had to ask six questions to get the correct answer: badminton.

1. Could you get the right answer by asking less questions than the team? Draw a flow chart to show how you would do it. Use circles for the team's questions and rectangles for the quiz master's answers. Begin with one of these questions:
   How many players? **or** How long each half?

2. Now draw a second flow chart to show how quickly you could get to the answer *hockey.* Use the information given in the table on page 25 to help you.

Redundancy in questioning. Interpreting and creating a flow chart. Using information presented as a table.

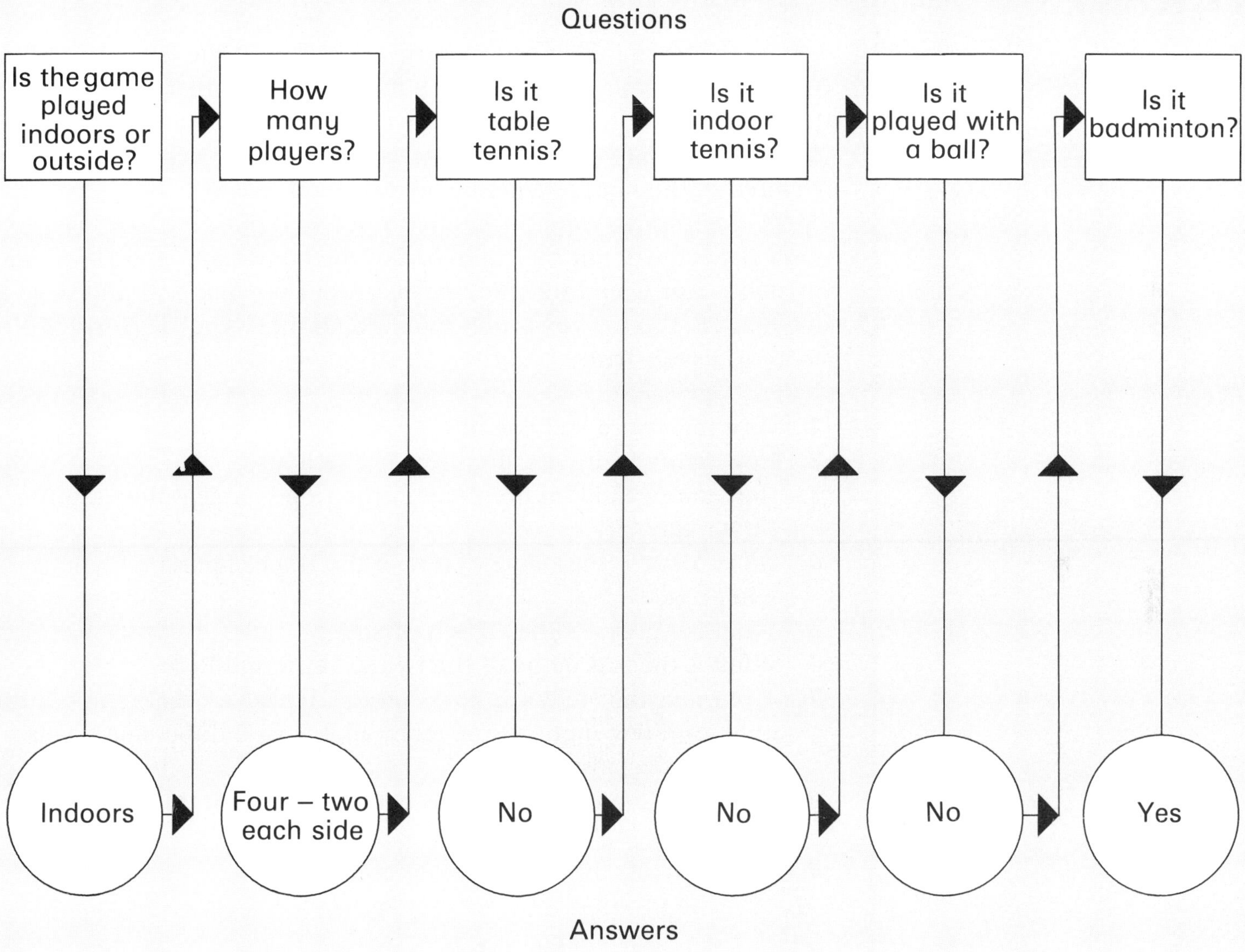
Questions
Is the game played indoors or outside?
How many players?
Is it table tennis?
Is it indoor tennis?
Is it played with a ball?
Is it badminton?
Indoors
Four – two each side
No
No
No
Yes
Answers

UNIT 10

Holidays

A The Hope children were excited. It was the summer holidays and their friends Liz and David were coming to stay.

However Mum looked a bit worried as she read the letter. Liz and David were coming on Tuesday, but she had promised Mrs. Porter, who lived next door, that she would have the twins, Rob and Mark, until Saturday so that Mrs. Porter could go to nurse her sick friend. Seven children in the house! Where would they all sleep?

"Oh, well," said Mum, "it's only for a few nights. I'm sure we can manage. We will put the camp bed in the boys' room and David and the twins can sleep there. You boys can put up your tent and sleep in the garden. I know you won't mind doing that! And Liz can share your room as usual, Jenny."

1. Give this text a suitable title.
2. How many bedrooms are there in the house?
3. How many children are there in the Hope family? How many boys? How many girls?
4. Do you know the name of any of the Hope children? If you do, what is it?
5. What is Mum's name? She is Mrs. □.
6. What is the last name of the twins, Mark and Rob?
7. Mum says that they can manage to sleep seven children because it's only for a few nights. How many nights would there be seven children sleeping there?
8. How can you tell that Liz has been to stay with the Hope family before?
9. Draw a plan showing where everyone slept.

Inferential comprehension. Converting prose to a plan.

THE HOPE CHILDREN'S FAMILY TREE

On the opposite page you were asked some questions about the Hope family. The best way to work out who the members of a family are and how they are related is by drawing a family tree. Here is a family tree for the Hope family, but some of the information is missing. If you read the text on the right you should be able to complete the family tree.

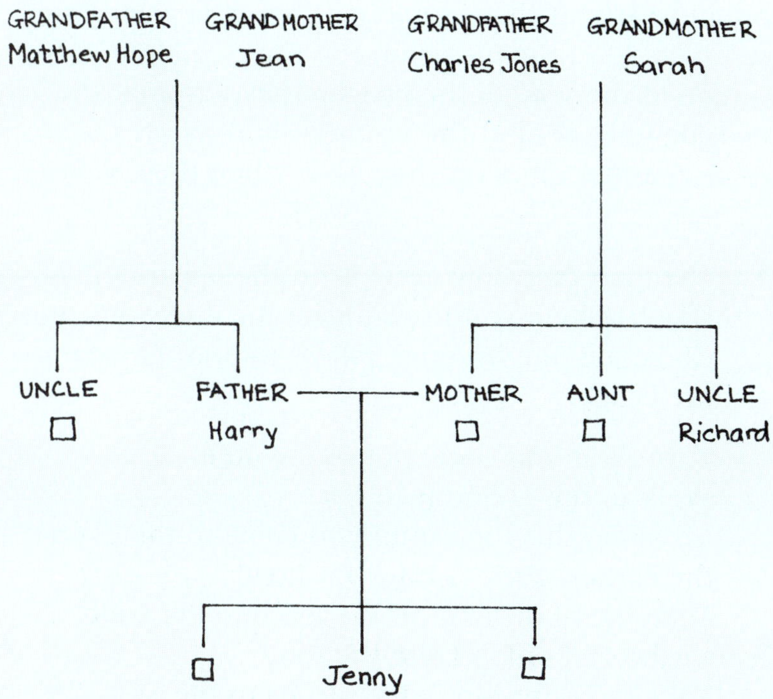

The first born son in the Hope family has always been called Matthew. This has been the case for hundreds of years. The first Matthew Hope was born in 1672 and there has been a Matthew in the family ever since.

Jenny's Mum was called after her mother, but this was because Mum's father liked the name very much. Jenny herself was called after her aunt.

Mum and Dad had great trouble in deciding what to call their youngest child. Mum wanted Dad's name but Dad said no, it was very confusing to have two people with the same name living in the same house. In the end Mum and Dad decided to call him after Dad's greatest friend. Funnily enough, it was the name of Mum's brother as well.

1. Copy the family tree into your book and complete it.
2. Answer these questions:
   a. How many uncles has Jenny Hope? What are their names?
   b. Who is the eldest of the Hope children?
   c. Who is older – Mum or Uncle Richard?
   d. Mum's last name is now Hope. What was her name before she married?
   e. Who is Jennifer Jones' sister?
   f. "I haven't got a brother." Who said that?
3. Draw your own family tree.

Family tree. Interpreting information presented in a form other than prose.

C The Hope family lived only a short distance from the sea, and in the summer they went swimming nearly every day.

The Hope children and their friends often went for a swim early in the morning, before breakfast. The first one awake would wake up the others and they would creep out of the house and down to the beach, their towels slung over their shoulders.

One summer, the Hope children had some new friends staying with them: Chris and Sandra. They were friends that the Hope children had made while staying with their grandparents in Scotland at Christmas.

Dad said that they must not wake Chris and Sandra early as they would be tired after their long journey. So in the morning, the Hope children drew a map of the way to the beach. They left it on the bedside table so that the visitors could follow the map and join them on the beach when they woke.

1. The map that they drew is on the opposite page. Use it to help you to complete the directions that Chris and Sandra must follow to find the way to the beach:

Turn □ as you come out of the gate.
Walk to the □ and turn left.
Go along this road until you come to the □ on the corner. Turn □ into Old Road.
Take the □ turning on the left into Pig Lane.
At the end of Pig Lane the road □.
Take the right fork which leads to the □.
From there you should be able to see us on the beach.

Converting a map into prose.

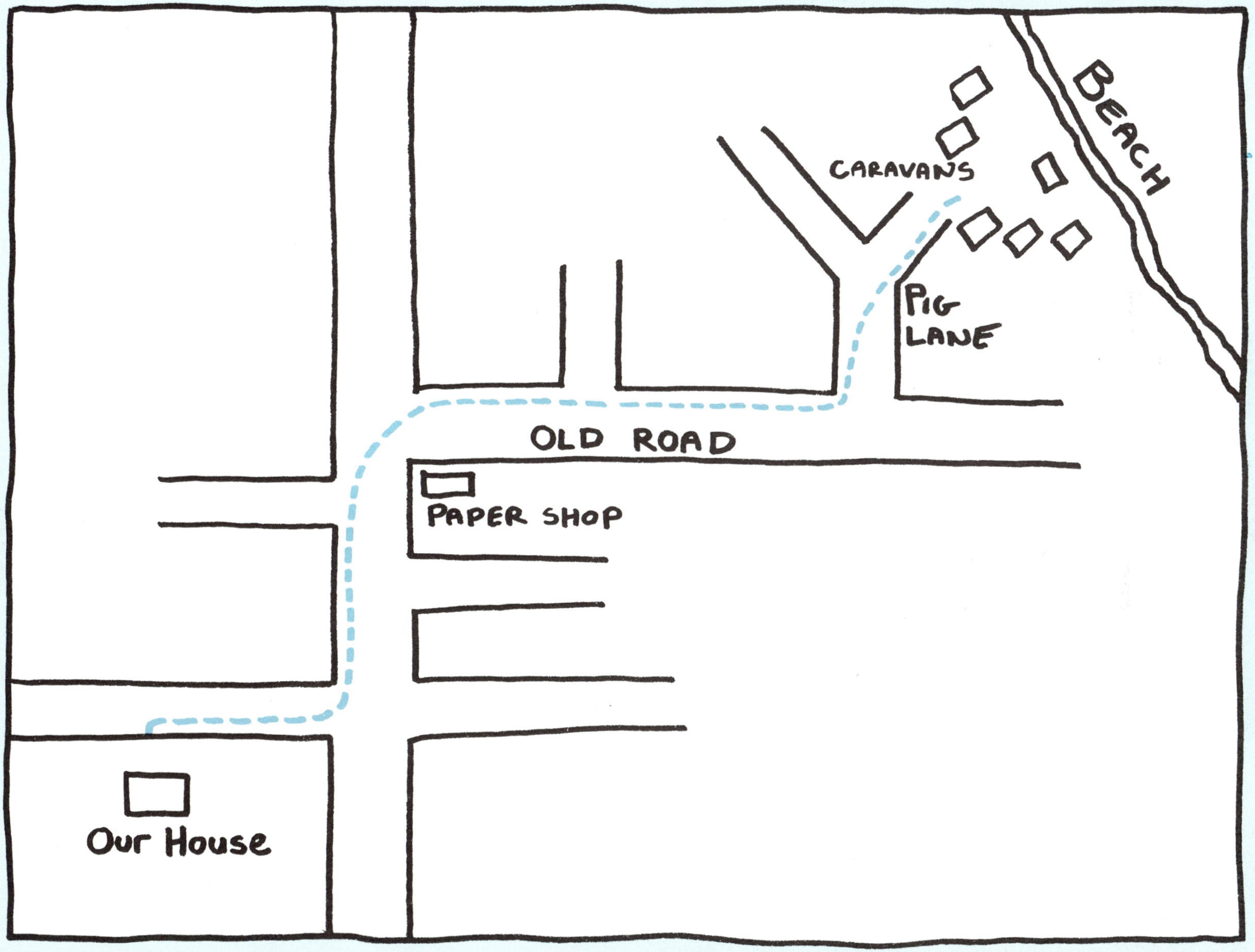
BEACH
CARAVANS
PIG LANE
OLD ROAD
PAPER SHOP
Our House

UNIT 11

Words and Pictures

A Look at the sketches in the boxes. They are all different. Only one sketch exactly fits the text written below. Which one is it?

The air was still. The wind, which had blown steadily for two days, had completely dropped away. The day had turned colder and it looked as though it might rain. The two men stood and stared at the house. Why did they feel so frightened? Surely nothing had changed? The curtains hung motionless at the windows. The car still stood in the drive. The only sign of life was the smoke rising from the chimney.

Evaluating information presented as sketches.

1.

2.

3.

4.

5.

6.

7.

8.

B Read this passage from *Alice in Wonderland:*

There was a table set out under a tree in front of the house, and the March Hare and the Hatter were having tea at it: a Dormouse was sitting between them, fast asleep, and the other two were using it as a cushion, resting their elbows on it, and talking over its head.

"Very uncomfortable for the Dormouse," thought Alice, "only, as it's asleep, I suppose it doesn't mind."

The table was a large one, but the three were all crowded together at one corner of it: "No room! no room!" they cried out when they saw Alice coming.

"There's *plenty* of room!" said Alice indignantly, and she sat down in a large armchair at one end of the table.

From *Alice's Adventures in Wonderland* by Lewis Carroll

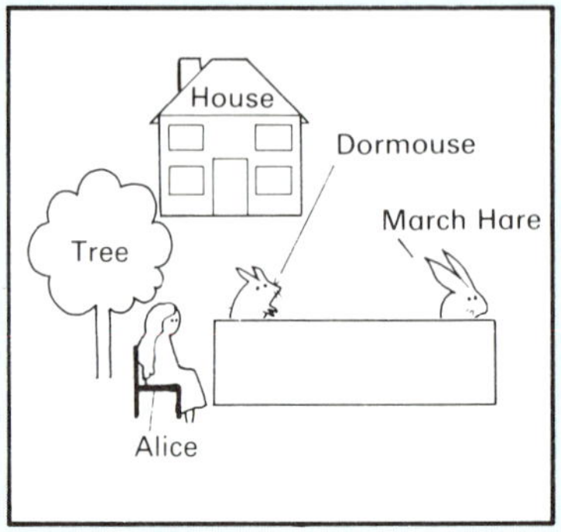

1.

2.

3.

4.

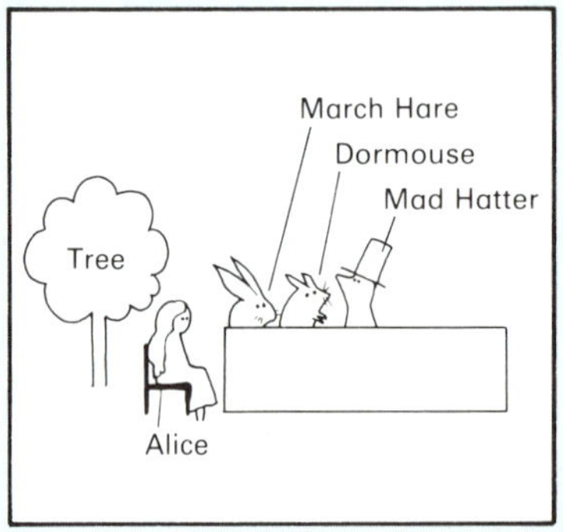

5.

6.

1. Look at the six boxes on the right. They show the information in the text as diagrams. But only one of these six diagrams is correct. Which one is it?
   Copy the correct diagram into your book. Put the number underneath.
2. Only one of the diagrams is correct, but there are at least two other ways in which the diagram could be drawn. Can you think of them? Draw in your book two more diagrams which will represent the text correctly.

Evaluating information presented as sketches. Finding alternative interpretations.

C

1. Read the text below. Then write down the four main differences between a guitar and a violin.

Guitar: This is played by plucking the strings with the right hand and by "stopping" the strings with the fingers of the left hand to vary the pitch. It usually has six strings. It is held across your lap.

Violin: This instrument is held beneath the chin and is usually played by drawing a bow across the four strings. It is smaller than a guitar.

2. Is this a photograph of a guitar or a violin?

3. Read the text below carefully. Then draw a diagram or plan in your book to show the position of:

the house, the stables, the woods, the lake, the paddock, the pony, Tom.

Beyond the wood, near the great lake, stood an old, old house. As Tom left the shadow of the trees, he saw the stolen pony grazing in the paddock which ran down to the lake. But it was not the pony that concerned Tom at this moment. He was looking for the horse thief. And, Tom decided, the best place to look for *him* was in the stables. He could see the end of a building that looked like the stables jutting out behind the silent old house.

Tom began to walk towards them.

UNIT 12

The Witch And The Cat

A Finding herself suddenly wealthy, the witch started going out every single night. She went to discos and late night snack bars. She went for fast drives on motor bikes and bought herself an expensive leather jacket with *Speed Cat* written on the back of it in gold studs.

Meanwhile, George, who was not a cat to complain about nothing (although *nothing* was exactly what he was getting for his supper each night) finally got fed up and left home. He took with him a small coffee table to sustain him on his journey and a bottle of tomato ketchup for flavouring.

When the witch found out that he had gone, she was very upset and put an advertisement in the paper which read:

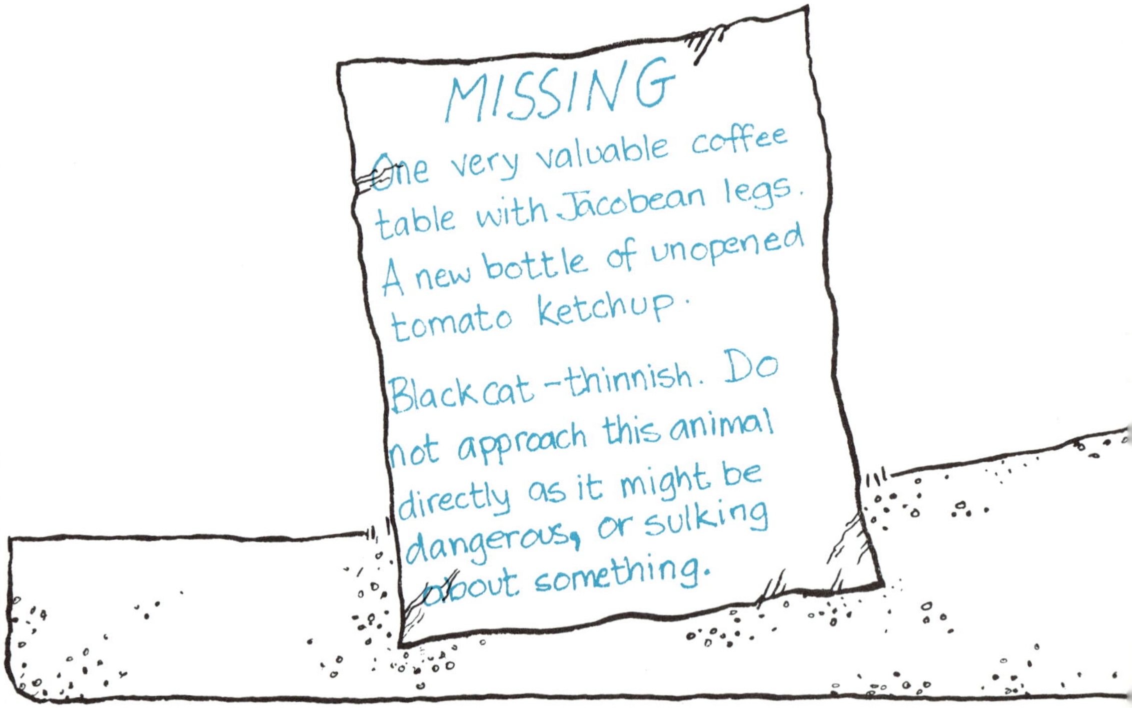

Main idea. Inferential comprehension.

Then she promptly forgot about George and carried on with her new life. But George didn't forget about himself. How could he?

He was lucky to find a comfortable dustbin for the night with a rainproof lid. He was even luckier to find it full of fish heads which made an excellent supper, allowing him to keep the coffee table and the tomato ketchup for leaner times.

From *Return of the Witch* by Margaret Stuart Barry

Now do this work in your book:

1. Write *one* sentence to explain what this text is about.
2. What did George take with him when he left home?
3. Why did he take these things?
4. What does "leaner times" mean?
5. We use all kinds of flavouring on, or in, our food. Write down *five* sorts of flavouring which you particularly like or which you often use.
6. Do you think the witch was really upset when she found that George was missing? If you do, say why. If you don't, say why not.
7. Pretend that it is *your* cat that is missing. Write an advertisement about your missing cat to put in the local paper.
8. What else could you do besides advertise to try to get your cat back? Write down two other things you might do.

B People are always losing things. At police stations, railway stations, bus stations and in big shops there are rooms full of things that people have forgotten and left behind.

Look at the table below. The articles listed in the table were all found in trains coming in to a big London railway station one day this year.

Victoria Station lost property office

Article	Number handed in	Train arrival	Platform number
umbrella	6	08.05	6
brief case	2	08.24	6
raincoat	3	08.37	6
shopping bag	4	10.54	5
purse	1	11.16	3
keys	3 (on a key ring)	11.30	4

By looking at the table, try to work out the answers to the following questions.

1. Which article was most often forgotten?
2. Why do you think this article might be most often left behind?
3. What do you think the weather was like on this particular day? Why do you think so?
4. Do you think it was a weekday or a Sunday? Give a reason for your answer.
5. Which article do you think would be the most upsetting to lose. Why?
6. What do you think most of the people were going to do who came on:
   a. the three earlier trains?
   b. the three later trains?

C Here is a further part of the story about the witch and the cat. George soon got tired of spending the night out in the cold and wet. Suddenly he remembered that Hatty, who was a friend of the witch, lived nearby. Hatty had a cat of her own and she was very generous with cat food. George decided to go and live with her. But Hatty was short of money. When she heard that there was work for her cats at the T.V. Centre, she took them there.

The Director of the Television Advertising Department was astonished to find only two cats waiting for him – and not very smart looking cats at that. He sent them off to the hairdressing department. And when they returned, looking almost as mangy as before, he said he supposed they would have to do. There were three saucers of cat food on the studio floor and the cats were supposed to choose number three, which was called Pussy's

Delight, with 3p off. But George pounced on the first cat food and gobbled it all up in about a second. Then he ate up the next saucerful, but didn't fancy Pussy's Delight, with 3p off, at all. Beelzebub, who understood they wouldn't get paid if they didn't choose the correct food, nibbled cautiously at Pussy's Delight, trying hard to disguise his disgust. But George soon discovered if he kept choosing the wrong saucers, they'd keep filling them up. Soon the whole floor was knee deep in wasted film and even the camera men, who thought it was funny at first, were getting fed up.

"No! No! NO!" bellowed the director. "Who interviewed that dumb cat?"

"You did", said the Continuity Girl.

Then Hatty the Howl, who was expecting to get £10,000 if the advert was successful, seized hold of George and hissed in his ear, "Why won't you eat number three?"

"It smells terrible," George hissed back.

"Can't you force yourself?" snapped Hatty.

George said that maybe he could, if they flavoured it with a bit of sawdust and a squirt of tomato ketchup.

"A bit of sawdust and a squirt of tomato ketchup," Hatty yelled. "If that isn't asking too much of you television lot."

Exasperated beyond all measure, the director hurled a large amount of sawdust and tomato ketchup into saucer number three and George devoured it with gusto. "Fantastic!" whooped the director, sweeping Beelzebub to one side and sacking him at the same time.

The sale of Pussy's Delight, with 3p off, rocketed, and cats all around the country were forced to eat it.

From *Return of the Witch* by Margaret Stuart Barry

Now answer these questions:

1. What was the job for the cats at the T.V. Centre?
2. Who was Beelzebub?
3. What did the Director do to try to make the cats look more presentable?
4. What was "Pussy's Delight"?
5. What does "3p off" mean?
6. Why was the floor knee deep in film?
7. **a.** What was Hatty known as?
   b. Why do you think she was called that?
8. Who do you think was more clever – George or Beelzebub? What makes you think so?
9. Do you think George did the cats all around the country a good turn by eating Pussy's Delight? If not, why not?

UNIT 13

Birdwatching

Here is a passage about the preparations you need to make before going birdwatching. It has been split up into a number of paragraphs. Each paragraph has one main idea unit, and a few important details.

Decide what each paragraph is about, and write a main heading for it in your book. Then write down the important details. Set it out like this:

Heading:
Details:

Make sure you pick out only the most important details. You are given some help with the first two paragraphs.

1. What you wear to go birdwatching depends on both the weather and the type of place you are going to visit. Most birds will see you long before you see them, so try not to attract their attention. Avoid bright colours and stick to the duller tones of brown, grey and dark green.

Heading: What to wear
Details: **a.** Try not to attract attention
b.

2. In summer wear lightweight clothes. You may be walking through rough countryside so make sure that they are fairly tough, or old.

Heading:
Details: Wear tough or old clothes

Summary: main idea and supporting details.

3. You can never trust the weather, so always take a light mac with you. If you have a pair of nylon over-trousers use them for walking in long grass after rain or in the early morning dew – the trousers can be rolled up and kept in your pocket when you are not using them.

4. Your notebook and pencil, a field guide and a map should all fit in the pockets of your mac or anorak. Other things, like an extra jumper, a thermos flask and sandwiches can be carried in a small rucksack. Line it with polythene to keep out the rain. If you are going to be sitting around for long periods, take a blow-up cushion as well – it can make bird-watching much more enjoyable!

5. Whatever the season, and particularly in winter, it is as well to be prepared for the cold. The most useful piece of clothing is a warm, weather-proof jacket with lots of deep pockets which either zip or button up. You can keep all the pieces of equipment you need to get at quickly and easily inside.

6. For rough and mountainous country strong walking shoes are best. In marshy areas wear wellingtons, although beware – they can be very tiring on really long walks.

From *Birdwatching* by Eileen Buckle

UNIT 14

Eating Out

A Read this text carefully. Then look at the table on the opposite page. It shows what everyone had to eat.

Friday came at last. This was the day that Paul had been looking forward to for a long, long time. He was going home after two months in hospital. Mum, Dad and Jane came for him at the end of the morning, after he had seen the doctor for the last time.

"Paul, we are going to have a treat because it is a special day," said Jane as soon as she saw him. "Daddy is taking us out for a meal!"

"Where would you like to go, Paul?" asked Dad.

Paul chose a place he had been to with his friend, Jim, when it was his birthday.

When they got there, they sat down at the table and looked at the menu. The waiter came up to take their order.

"Paul, what about you?" said Dad. "Soup?"

"Yes, please."

"Jane, what will you have?"

"I'll have the fruit juice."

"Mother?"

"I'll have the same."

"Right. We'll have two soups and two fruit juices. Now: main course. There's fish and chips, roast lamb and steak pudding. Paul, you mustn't have meat. Mother?"

"I'll have fish too please."

"And roast lamb for me please," said Jane.

"Good. That's one lamb, one steak pudding and two fish. And ices to follow, please."

Inferential comprehension.

1. Copy the table below into your book.
2. Complete the table by referring to the text.

Table to show what everyone had to eat

	diners			
menu	Mum	Dad		Paul
fruit juice			√	
				√
fish and chips	√			
			√	
steak pudding				
	√		√	

AT THE SPORTS HALL

It was Nicola's birthday. Instead of having a party, she chose to take four friends to the Sports Hall for the afternoon. They had a marvellous time. At the end of the afternoon, they all went to the refreshment room. Nicola asked them what they wanted to eat and drink.

"I'll take your orders for the drinks first," she said.

"I'd like a Coke, please," said Joe.

"Me too," said Sharon.

"I think I'll have lemonade," said Stuart.

"A glass of milk for me, please," said Kim.

"Come and help me Joe," said Nicola. "I'll collect the drinks and you can bring the food. Orders for food please!"

"Sausages and chips," said Sharon and Stuart together.

"Baked beans on toast for me," said Nicola.

"And for me," said Kim.

Nicola and Joe went to the self-service counter and filled their trays. Joe collected two plates of baked beans on toast, one of hamburgers and chips and two of sausages and chips. Nicola followed him and paid for the food and drink out of the money her parents had given her. On her tray she had two Cokes, two lemonades and a glass of milk.

1. Copy the table below into your book and complete it by looking back at the text.

2. Give your table a title.

food and drink / children						

C Nicola's birthday was in April. She was lucky because her birthday was on a Saturday this year. Her friend Joe was lucky too. He was just three days older than Nicola and the children broke up for the Easter holidays the day before his birthday. The last day of term was April 13th.

Look at the calendar and then answer the questions below:

April

Sun	Mon	Tue	Wed	Thu	Fri	Sat
				1	2	3
4	5	6	7	8	9	10
11	12	13	14	15	16	17
18	19	20	21	22	23	24
25	26	27	28	29	30	

1. The 19th of April falls on which day?
2. What date is the first Wednesday in April?
3. When is Joe's birthday?
4. When is Nicola's birthday?
5. Joe has a party on the Saturday after his birthday. When is that?
6. Nicola said: "My birthday is a week from tomorrow". On which day was she speaking?
7. The Easter holidays last a fortnight. On which date do the children go back to school?
8. Copy this bar graph into your book. Ask the other children in your class when their birthday is and complete the bar graph.
Then answer the questions below.

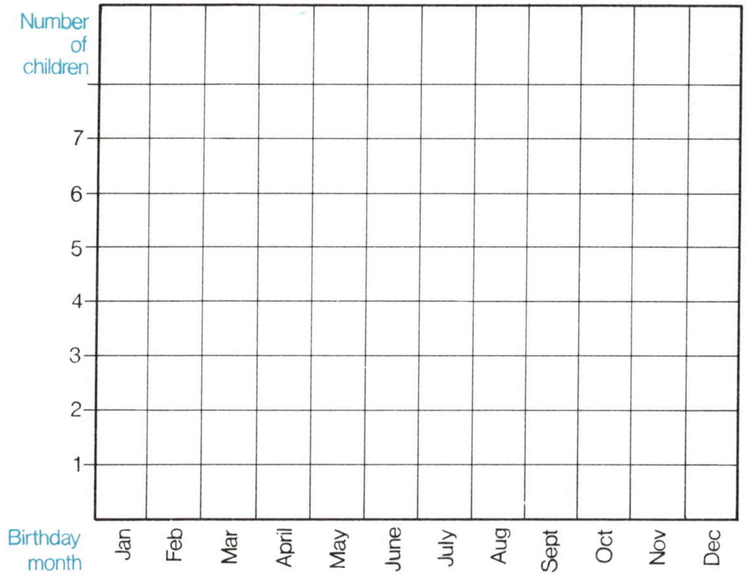

a. Most schools are closed for the whole of the month of August. How many children in your class have their birthdays in August?

b. In which month do most children have birthdays in your class?

c. In which month do fewest or no children have birthdays?

d. Were more children born in the first half of the school year (September – February) or in the second half (March – August)?

UNIT 15

Machines Used For Rescue

"All over the world machines are used to rescue people who are in danger."

This first sentence tells you what the unit is about. The keywords in the sentence are **machines** and **rescue**. So the title for these pages could be **MACHINES USED FOR RESCUE**.

Each paragraph tells you about different machines and the work they do. Find a heading for each paragraph and make a list of the important details. The first paragraph is done for you.

1. The wail of an ambulance siren can often be heard in the streets of large towns. The ambulance on its way to an accident carries oxygen masks and cylinders. It also carries equipment known as a sucker unit which can pump food and liquid from the stomach.

Heading: Ambulances

Detail: Machinery which is part of the equipment of an ambulance:

a. siren

b. oxygen masks and cylinders

c. sucker unit

2. A 999 call often brings out the Fire Brigade. Fire engines carry the very largest appliances. A powerful pump forces the water through the hoses. The power-operated ladders rescue people from high buildings. The acetylene cutting gear is used to release people who are trapped in crashed cars.

Heading:

Details: **a.**

b.

c.

3. Mining underground is always dangerous. Every mine has workers specially trained for rescue work.

A rescue worker does not breathe the mine air which may be poisonous. Instead he uses a cylinder of oxygen strapped to his back and a mask which covers his face. He also has an electric light fixed to his protective head gear and a Davy lamp which warns him when he reaches poisonous air in the mine.

Heading:
Details: **a.**
b.
c.

4. Lifeboats are stationed along all the busy coasts of the world. The boats and their crews are ready at any time of the day or night to go to the rescue of ships in trouble at sea. Lifeboats carry many safety devices such as searchlights, signalling lamps, radar, radio telephone and a line-throwing pistol which can shoot a line from the lifeboat to a boat in distress.

Heading:
Details: **a.**
b.
c.
d.
e.

5. Most aircraft have fixed wings. Helicopters have rotor blades which are spinning wings. Helicopters are most useful in rescue work. They can remain hovering over a disaster or accident whilst the victims are winched by cable to the safety of the helicopter. By using this winch helicopters are able to lift people off mountains, or cliff faces or pluck them out of the sea. They can rescue people trapped on top of burning buildings. They can take the place of a crane, lifting girders and other heavy objects.

Helicopters are often used to "rescue" crops. Insects can damage crops. On very large farms, helicopters carrying special spraying equipment are used to get rid of them. The helicopters fly over the fields and spray pesticide on the insect pests eating the crops below.

Heading:
Details: **a.**
b.

ACTIVITY OR SKILL INVOLVED		UNIT NUMBER 1	2	3	4	5	6	7	8	9	10	11	12	13	14	15
Search																
Classifying																
Questioning																
Dictionary/Reference																
Comprehension																
Literal																
Inferential																
Evaluative																
Sequencing																
Summarising																
Format																
Prose																
Diagram	interpreting															
	completing															
	creating															
Map	interpreting															
	creating															
Flow	interpreting															
	creating															
Table	interpreting															
	completing															
	creating															
Plan	completing															
	creating															
Bar Graph	creating															